The 11:11

Poems like pickled emotions

VALKYRIE

(Dr. Vandana V.)

Made with ❤ on the Notion Press Platform

www.notionpress.com

Dedicated to

the earth, water, fire, air, and space,

for making my world.

Contents

Acknowledgments

This book is a tribute to every soul that has moved me and led me to poetry:

My father, the enigma that he is. Humble as the flame of a candle, he's always been the spark in my life. My mother, the paradox to enigma! She has forever been my fearless warrior clad under the veil of innocence; I could never be anything, if not for her.

My dearest darlings, Kauser and Namrata: each one from a different dimension of my amoebic life, these women never give up on me. The number of awesome friends I've met through them is endless. The number of times they've saved me from myself is insane.

The people in my life! Strangers who'd befriended me, loved me, shown me their scars and comforted mine, shared laughs, dreams and ideologies, and inspired me to write. I owe you more than just a cup of tea. Some day!

Peace and Hugs.

1. THE SOCIAL TOXICITY

Humans are all created equal

Yet some of us come in the fateful design..

That's stared at by creepy smiles

That shall only sneak but not dare shine..

Fearing dark corners or loud crowds,

There's no place we're safe or free.

Despite decades of independence,

We only dream of big dreams or degree.

Forget wanderlust, forget the sandal lost,

Even the street's end threatens my kin.

When will this massacre end? When can I breathe?

Should I have a girl child, And then fret in despair?

For she will be in fear too, She will be glared at..

Because unlike the glorified feminine idols,

We're real women, thin or fat.

We cook, we clean, we love and care,

We fight, we scream but only darkness shall fare.

2. THE WOOF OF HONOUR

One day I met Scooby-Doo (named so by me)

Dry blood still lingering on one ear,

His scars had stories to tell, if you'd hear.

His heart seemed to pace, his lungs in a race,

So still and calm, giving company to a lonely stranger..

He was comforted by the familiarity, no harm or danger.

Guarding, guiding, playful mate..

You wouldn't dare to tease his temper.

With a tiny claw on the edge of each soft paw,

He could rip anything into bone and tender..

I wonder if it was the same soul that fought for food and honour.

3. THE LEATHER JACKET

People talk of doves and eagles

but I grew up watching bats more closely.

And unlike their love lessons and motivational speeches of the others,

the eerily loud silence of the bats always kept me intrigued.

The flying foxes attack picturesque sunsets,

hundreds of them in batches,

mocking the naive lovers of the purple skies.

With no feathers but wings of leather,

they gush and rush across the shy mountains..

Like young bikers on wild terrains, showing off their leather jackets and shiny metal tanks,

as if they dint care who ruled the world.

But just like all the rude rowdies, they'd slow down,

stuttering at 50 frames per second, and secretly blush

in front of the mystic moon.

And she ignores it all royally yet respectfully,

continuing to blithe and bask all by herself

in the luminous darkness.

Her confidence tearing down egos,

her charm makes stone cold hearts warm.

Independent, bold and gorgeous,

she seems as if she needs no one,

or does she?

4. WINGS OF UNCERTAINITY

Half wing up, half wing down,

Flying across a stranger town,

Half way past the globe blue green,

Flying with the wind and a flock of my own,

Half unsure, half compass drawn,

Gliding in the sky's embrace.

Off from one home to another,

Dancing to new dreams on the edge of horizon.

5. THE ECLIPSES

Some flowers, fragrant whispers in the breeze,

Some tears, glistening like morning dew,

Some scars and stardust woven with ease,

Warm flesh and bones and a heart of stone,

Mostly poetic, always dramatic,

Like a queen without a tiara or throne,

The recipe of a human antique.

Her tan shining in moonlight's embrace,

And a smile that never fades away,

Drifting between Kafka's existential dread

And Macbeth's ambition where dreams decay,

Her soul roams lost behind the many facades,

Within each mask, there's a story she'd never say.

6. LE ROUGE

Everytime I see the color Red

It fills my heart with the questions I most dread..

Is it the universe sending signals to my head??

Is it love in the air or danger ahead??

Pretty as it looks, it feels like wounds and bloodshed..

Fierce, freaky, dangling on a silken thread..

My blood dances like butterflies and bugs and ants fire-fed

The million souls jumping like monkeys in the bed

And into the ocean of tears they lead

Bumping, bouncing,

sinking in tea like biscuit and bread.

The anxiety is real, the panic surreal

The hopeless romantic is pitching at the next idyll

No! Dont go there! My angels yell

Dont look into those honey eyes!

Dont trust those deathly melodies..

You'll slip and fall and hit rock bottom,

And loose yourself in the endless quantum!

The margins have diminished,

No returns' worth the risk..

I'm now a monk once banished

From the land of pink hearts with an asterisk.

7. OF ROSES, REGRET AND RED FLAGS

Midnights are no more dark,

Not dark enough..

A million thoughts chase my ignorance

"Was I never good enough..?"

They scream at me in chaotic silence..

For when was enough ever enough!

Scathing tears find their way through reflections,

The light in the end splitting in all dimensions,

the end feels close enough.

If love can’t give me peace,

I'm better off away from war..

I don’t like roses anymore,

I'm no more taking the scar..

Drenched in despair, I walk into my dreams,

My bags full of regrets and memories, fair and foul,

"Well, nothing lasts forever" said a random graying soul.

And I hear the hollow voice of reassurance that the

pestilence shall end..

Soon there would be no feeling you cannot mend..

Nothing can break you anymore,

nothing can fix you either,

No sane love would you ever attract,

nothing sparsely lovable either.

8. HAVOC WRECKED HUMOUR

Life is funny

I'm living a life that's a dream to many,

I dread waking up each day to the clockwork and clowns,

Faking a smile, hiding the frown.

I often regret sharing thoughts, if any,

And have now befriended the lump in my throat..

Let me sink in the misery,

I'd rather not drift, or float.

Life is so funny

Countless souls stay blocked across endless networks,

Yet I'd been longing since forever for the One

Who'd sit with me comfortably in silence,

But only darkness turned out to be that close companion

except the stars shining on the horizon.

For in the dark there's no demon I fear,

and no one can see my turmoil and tears.

Life is funny

I watch people make a curry or a joke,

laughing at the curse words in beeps..

And then go back to bed crying out of the loneliness,

trying to put myself to sleep.

34 and unmarried, my kin think I'm a cold, heartless witch,

And I embrace this guise; their prying eyes would twitch.

Life is funny,

It mocks me with a witty giggle

as I fight imaginary courtroom arguments with God..

Calling him out for every uncalled-for feeling..

Why show me dreams that were destined to fates odd?

And He just watches from above,

Unmoved by my emotional act..

Sentencing me forever to the cursed pact.

9. THE OFFSHORE BALLAD

In the sea of a billion souls, where shadows entwine,

Echoes of laughter weave through silence divine.

What if, in the silence, love slips from our grasp?

Yet, in the stillness, we learn to unclasp.

For beauty resides in the spaces between,

And peace remains a myth unseen.

10. TO THE MOON AND BACK

Too real to be true,

Like cinematic cue.

Giving, forgiving,

Dead on days, leaving nights for living.

Adamant and hesitant too,

Distant yet constant,

It's always me for you.

For the kind of love I always gave

Is it too much to crave?

11. THE C MINOR

The smell of new books,

Washed, conditioned and sundried clothes,

A view of the sea shore,

some serial lights

and an automatic room freshner,

Home-made cake,

my favourite chocolate,

Whisky smuggled in to the house in a sipper

Plugged in the best noise cancelling headphones,

I surrounded myself with all the things I love.

Yet the sound of a minor third

broke my heart all over again.

For the millionth time, yes.

Pretendable, the fool that I was,

always catching feelings from the silence between cords.

Helpless, I cannot deny,

I prayed to all the gods..

To give me reason, show me a sign,

I cannot get over the madness to have 'mine'.

The song ends,

some tears dry and others hang off the chin..

Winter winds rush through the curtains

And the ghosts in my head leave in the interim,

Until the next C minor shall begin.

12. THE LUCIFER EFFECT

Sometimes I come across this creature

Wandering in a transient cave in my soul..

The fugitive seems harmless at first encounter

And slowly turns green, venomous and foul.

Honest but brutal, her love is often misgiven.

She carries flowers vibrant and delicate

From the cactus she bred in her lonely garden..

And lends them to the one confused delinquent

She begs to nurture but warns of the torture

Because Oh!! Flowers wither but thorns thrive..

And they'd give you wounds that last forever

Like a wicked curse until you survive.

She pleads guilty of her vile words

Love was all she ever wanted..

But she only found the rustic swords

Alas! My soul remains haunted.

13. THE TANGIBLES

Times have changed,

being detached is the new cool.

I now keep souvenirs and memorabilia closer to my heart

while the memories are preferably muted.

What's the difference you may ask..

I swear, it's cute and weighs less on the heart.

Over the recent past, I've gathered a lot of things

ranging from a screwdriver to a pine cone

each one of them means a lot:

stories of love, friendship, travel, and parts of me.

And every time I come across any of these tangibles

it is sure to send a rush of chemicals through my blood..

Catalyzing the emotions wrecking my mind.

And all it takes is to hold on for a few seconds..

seconds of long, chaotic calmness..

which help me build enough strength to put it away,

and let my thoughts dissolve into thin air.

EPILOGUE

And the tangibles continue to hide in plain sight,

Unlike the people, they remain mine until a lifetime.

14. UNCONDITIONED

I have that one unconditioned friend

Who trusts me more than I do myself.

She prays for my prayers to be answered

And prays for me through all my times tough..

She cries with me at my agony

She holds me tight when tides get rough..

And rejoices in my every tiny victory.

I've been through falls and setbacks,

I've had my share of dubious luck

And although my choices traumatized her too

She never gave up on this ugly duck.

If I could ever paint the world for her

I'd make it a pretty purple

I'd add all things small, soft and pretty..

And some lillies, wine and chocolate truffle.

Talking to her is always a relief

We talk of drama: Korean, Chinese, Turkish, and others

And although I see myself just like a goofy house elf

With her I always feel like the Wright Brothers.

Trying and failing and still trying to fly

For the love of the differences and of our mothers.

15. ERROR: PERFECT

The most intricate braid that only lives until its untied..

The delicate froth of coffee that still lingers on the emptied cup..

That one loud friend of the protagonist -

blurred, muted, and scooted aside in moments that matter the most.

The liked but never chosen one;

the one that's too much or just not enough.

The unwavering slope between the peaks and the trough.

The best that's never bought..

The unsaid that's never sought..

Has to be mere luck or sheer randomness,

Or a biased God who made this mess.

Why else would the sun give its light to the moon

just to be loathed for its extremeness?

16. IN THE PINK OF DUSK

She stood there watching the sky turn pink,

Whether it was rage or diffidence she was yet to decide.

A faint star in the far horizon showed up like a wink

and a smile to let the maladies hide.

Words crowded in her head like people in a busy lane,

No matter how much she tried, she failed to filter a few.

Avoiding even the slightest thought insane,

the nomad stood still without a clue.

They told her "believe in the process!"

But the process had alternate possibilities.

A familiar felony of the wretched cupids,

Twisted in fate's conspiracies.

What was broken could never be mended,

No magical stardust came to the rescue.

Shattered beyond reason or apology,

she gave up trying to stick or sew.

The white winged side kick had taken a bullet to the head,

The red tailed genius sighed, exhausted,

No more argument on the heart's destiny.

It was her favorite dream screwed.

Her feet sank in the wet sand, her hair danced in the wind,

She had found peace in the chaos, waiting for the end.

17. WHITE LILLIES AND WHITE LIES

Clear skies and whistling winds,

The whitest lilies and a calm mind.

So much for a passed storm,

Finding peace in denial, so warm.

Tranquility is often misinterpreted,

Defamed in the name of grief.

Just as an unassuming smile is misled into tears cold,

Pondering on the truths beyond belief.

18. HUES

It's always there

Just around the corner

It's warmth is contagious,

It's strength is inspiring.

You just don't see it strolling in slow motion

Or freezing in glamour and glitz.

No violins, no roses, no poster poses..

Just love in its million hues.

Raw and Unscripted,

It's rebellion fatal..

Endless and Fair,

Slight yet factual..

Love is always in the air.

19. LE BELLA CIAO

"When one door closes, another opens" they said,

But when one show was cancelled,

we'd set up a makeshift theater -

Cutting lines, Skipping stares,

we were three epitomes of drama but fine.

From delayed trains and unreal deadlines

To forgiving order declines..

Manifesting the cosmic energies in every sign

To find the perfect place to chill and dine..

Giggling and gossiping like girls aged nine,

With smiles brighter than the moon's sunshine..

Living for holidays, haleem and midnight desserts divine.

Crazy girlfriends, they fill the voids in my heart,

And calm the blood in my veins..

My guardian angels, with lip gloss and brains.

The Optics of my world

EPILOGUE

EPILOGUE

EPILOGUE

EPILOGUE

EPILOGUE

EPILOGUE

www.ingramcontent.com/pod-product-compliance
Lightning Source LLC
LaVergne TN
LVHW091239150826
845673LV00003B/1217